Rose Tattoo Coloring Book

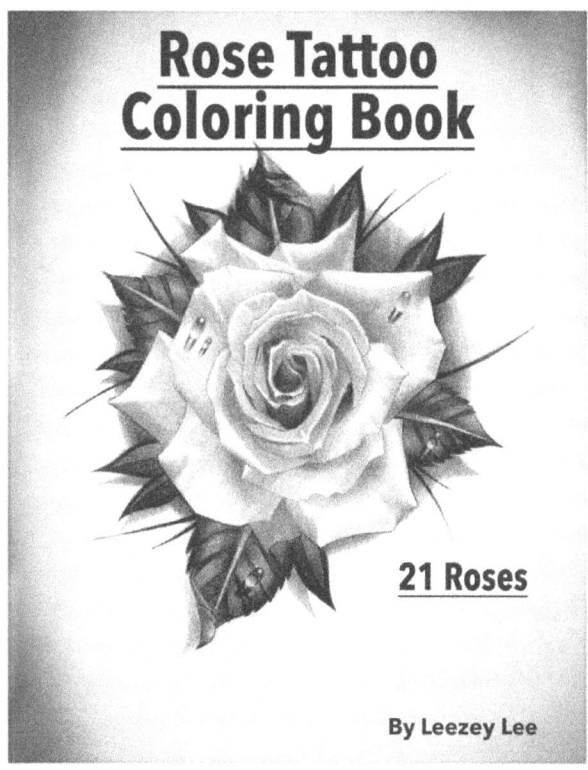

Leezey Lee

Rose Tattoo Coloring Book

Copyright © 2021 Leezey Lee

All rights reserved.

ISBN: 9798529721216

DEDICATION

CONTENTS

	Acknowledgments	1
1	Rose 1	Pg 3
2	Rose 2	Pg 9
3	Rose 3	Pg 15
4	Rose 4	Pg 21
5	Rose 5	Pg 27
6	Rose 6-12	Pg 33
7	Rose 13	Pg 39
8	Rose 14	Pg 45
9	Rose 15	Pg 51
10	Rose 16	Pg 57
11	Rose 17-21	Pg 63
	About the Author	68

ACKNOWLEDGMENTS

ROSE 1

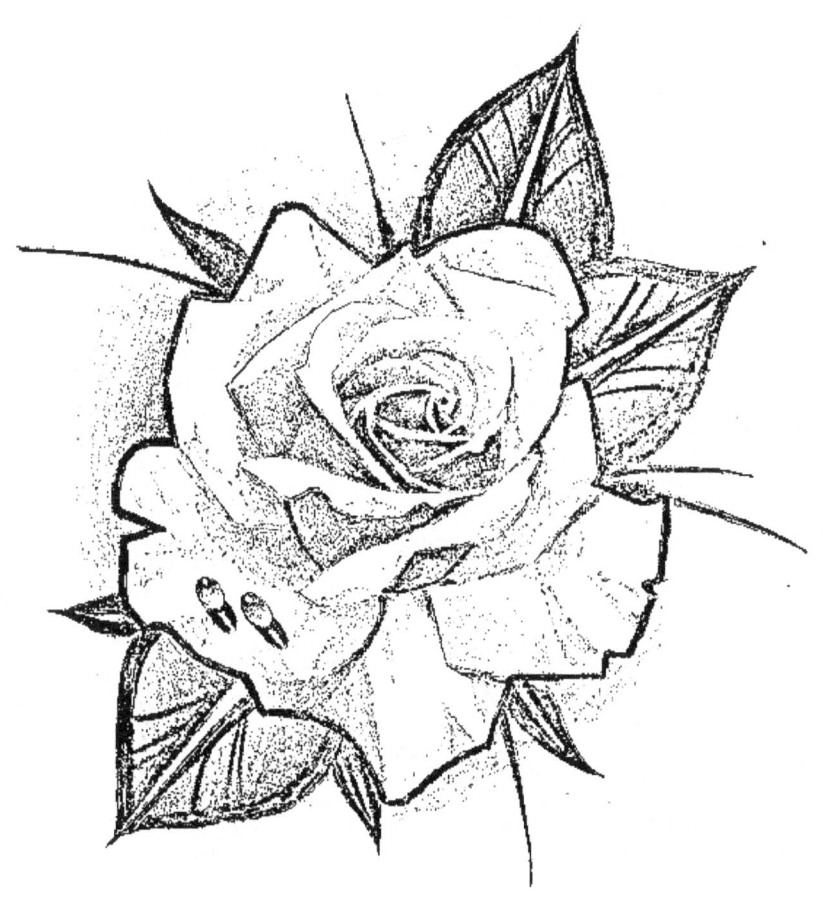

BOOK TITLE

Blank

ROSE 1

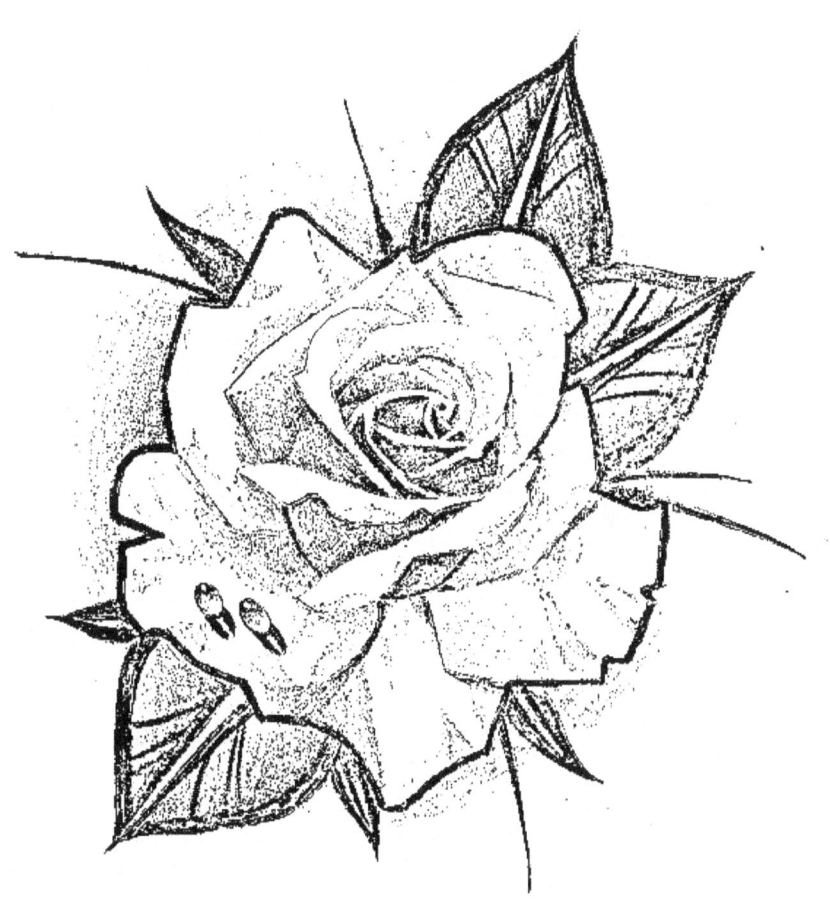

BOOK TITLE

Blank

ROSE 1

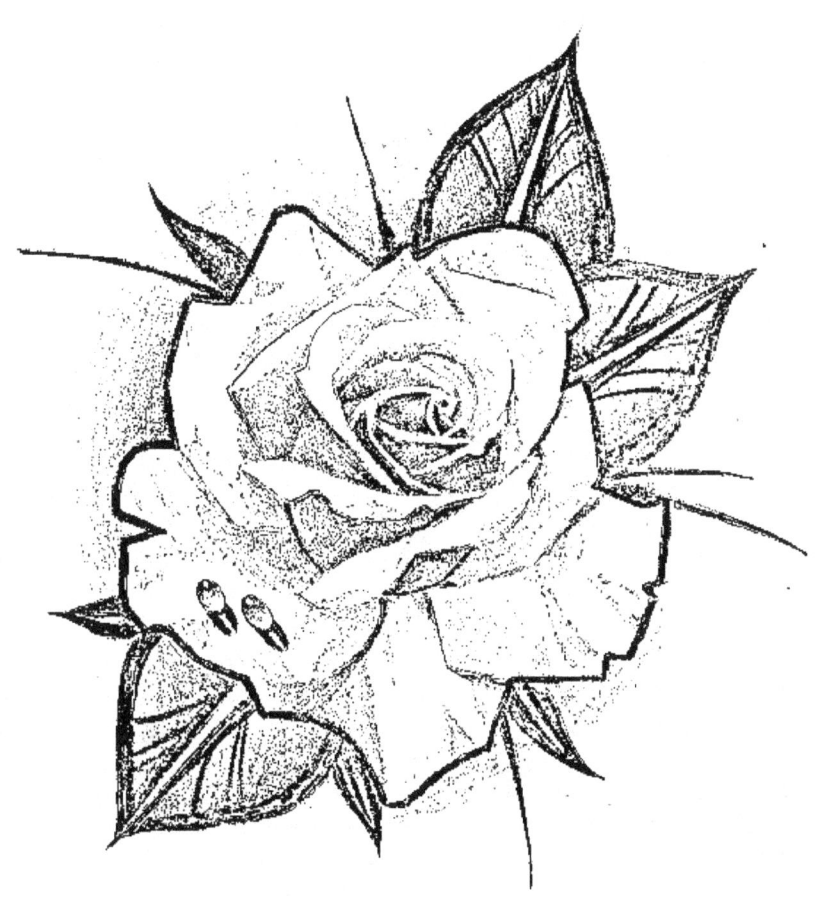

BOOK TITLE

Blank

ROSE 2

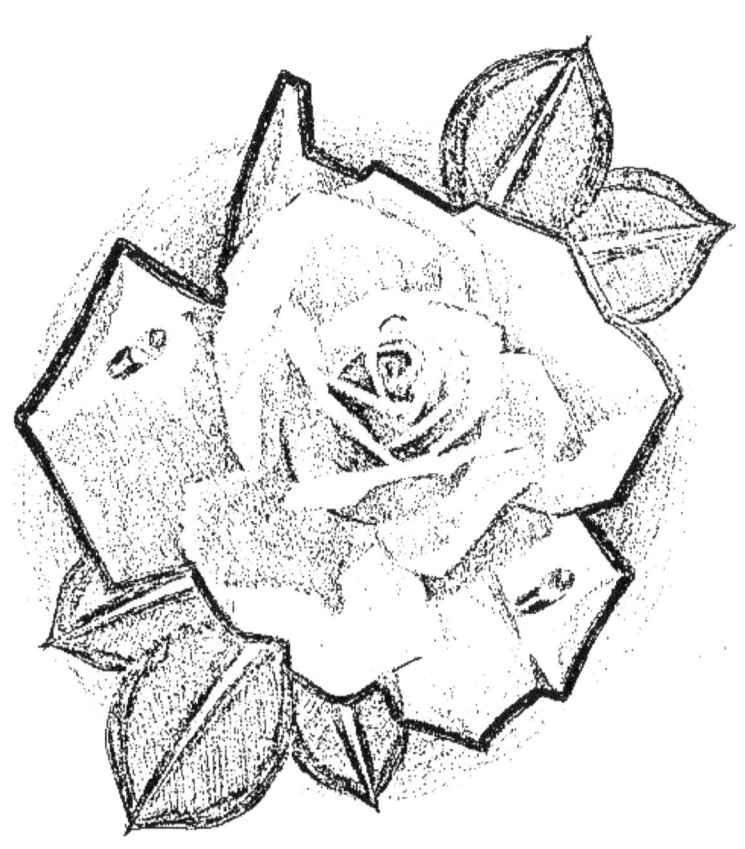

BOOK TITLE

Blank

ROSE 2

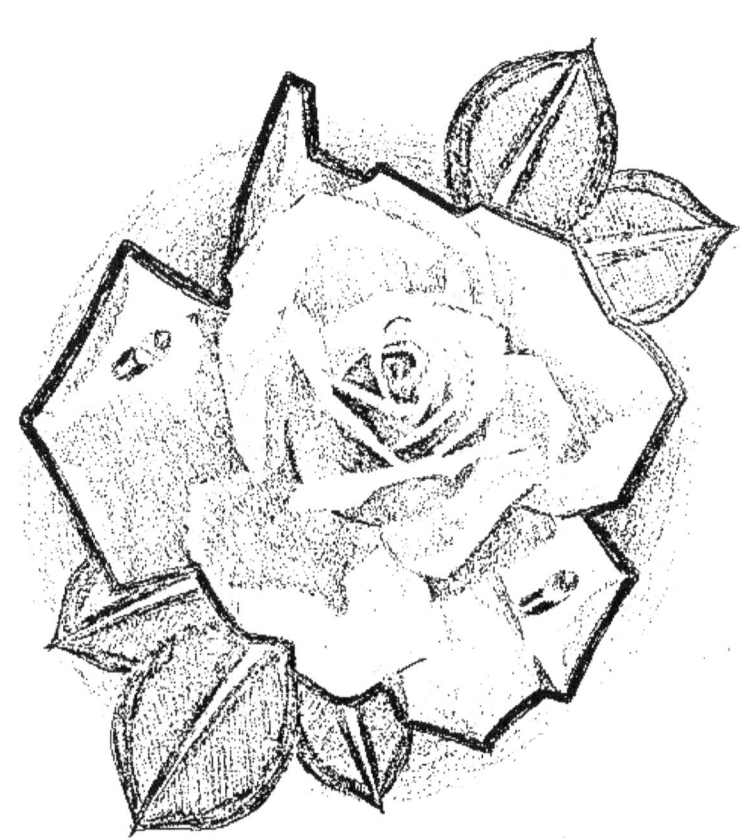

BOOK TITLE

Blank

ROSE 2

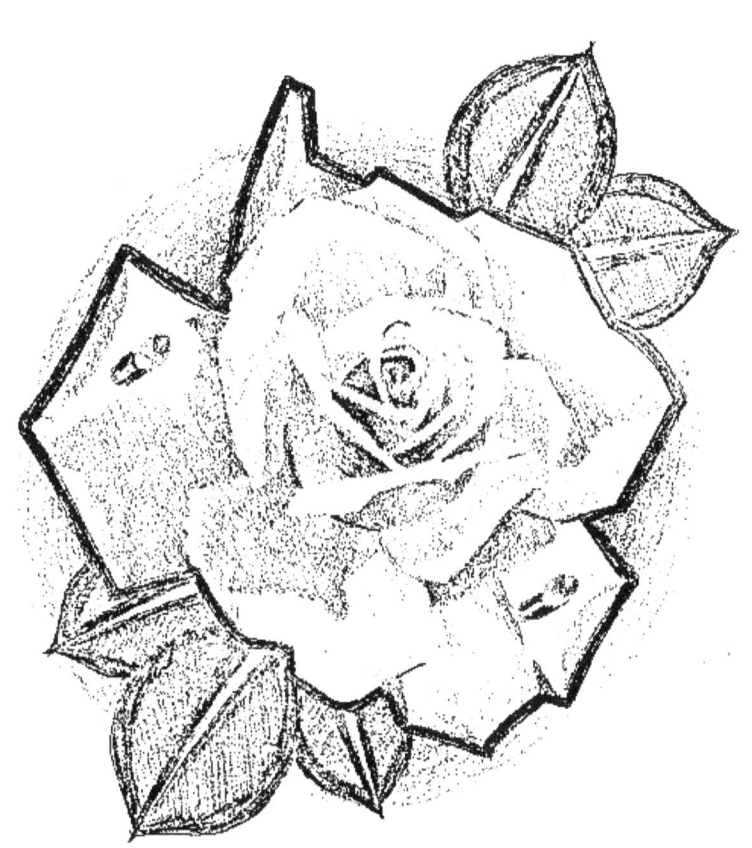

BOOK TITLE

Blank

BOOK TITLE

ROSE 3

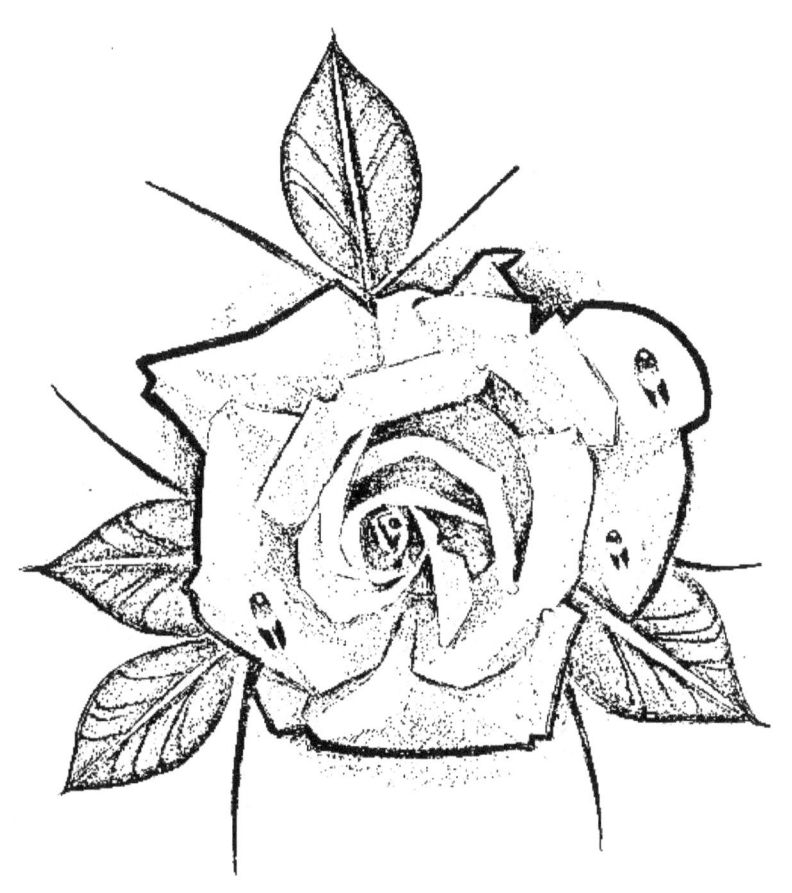

BOOK TITLE

Blank

BOOK TITLE

ROSE 3

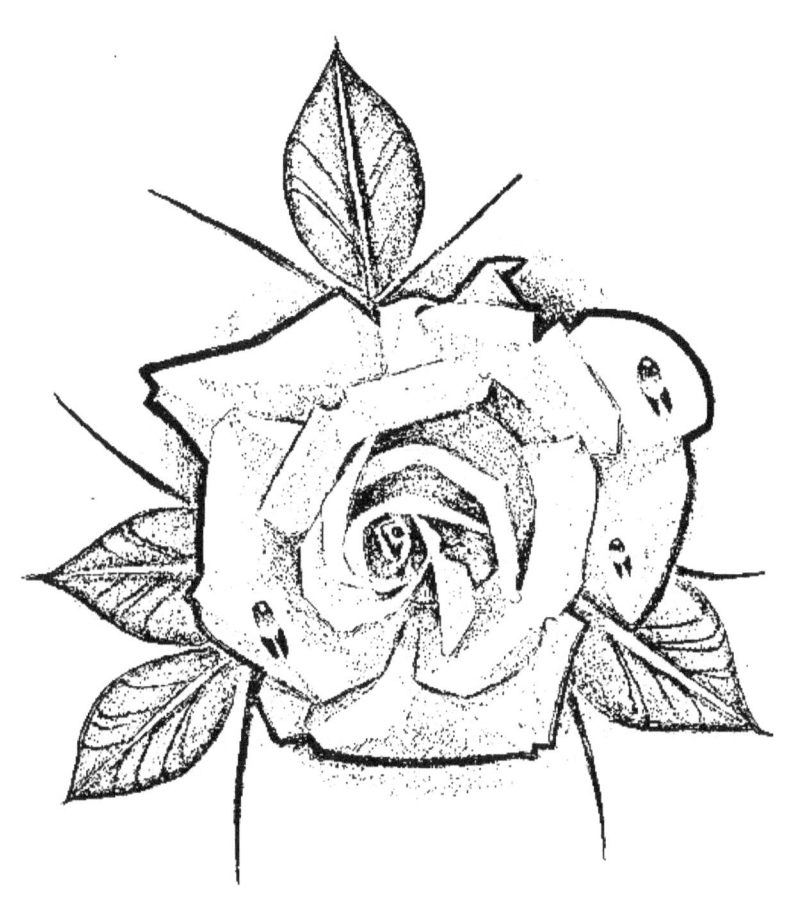

BOOK TITLE

Blank

ROSE 3

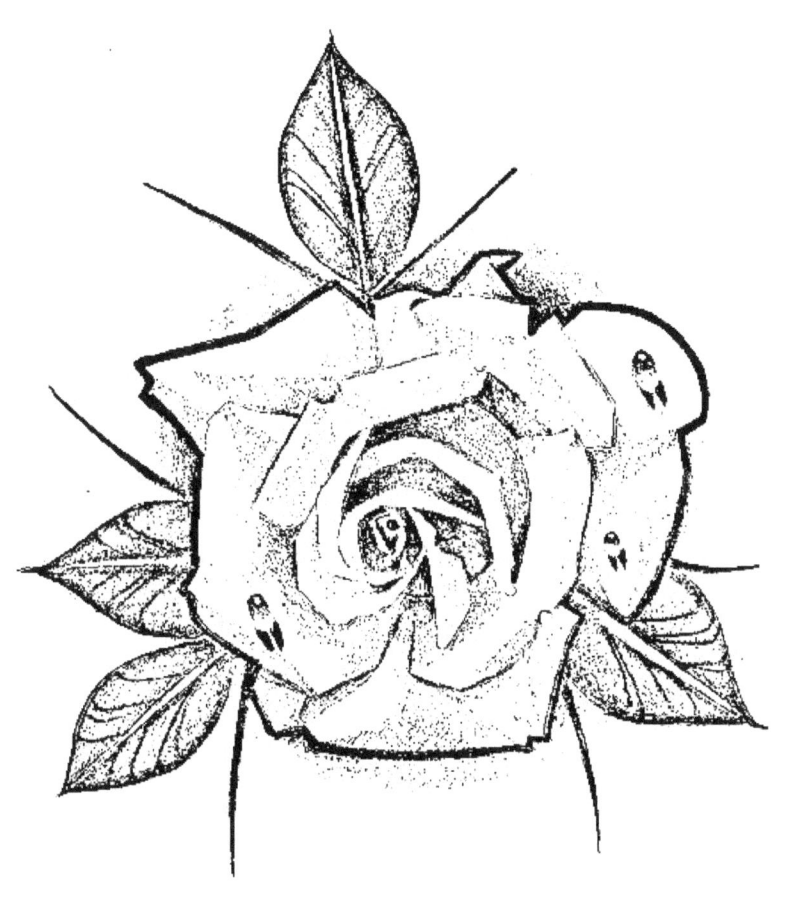

BOOK TITLE

Blank

ROSE 4

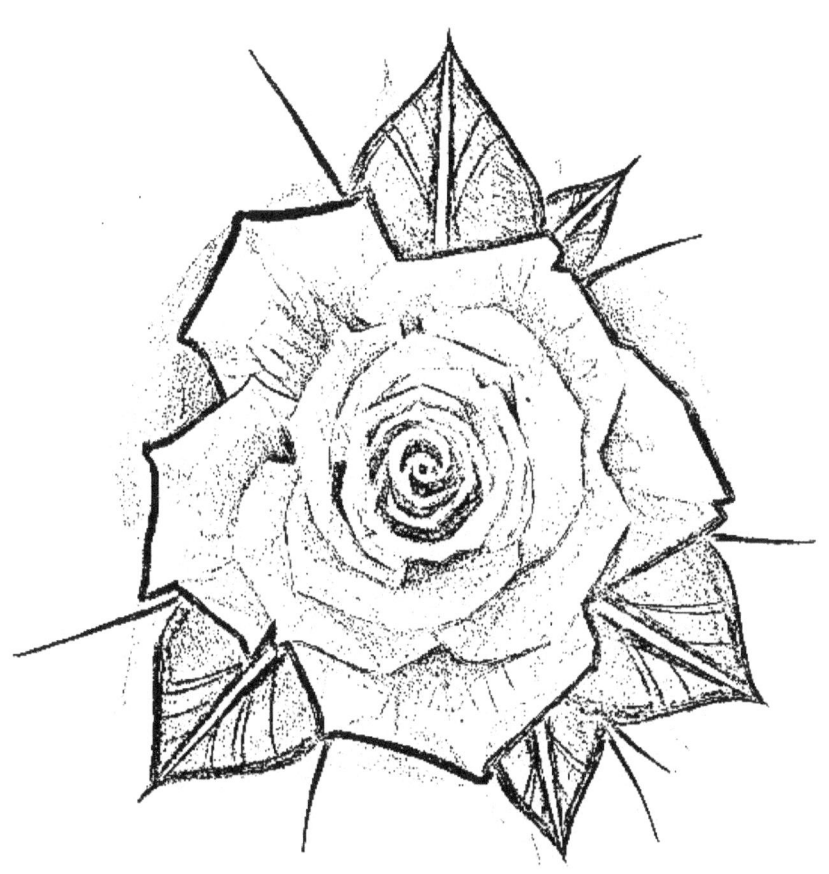

BOOK TITLE

Blank

BOOK TITLE

ROSE 4

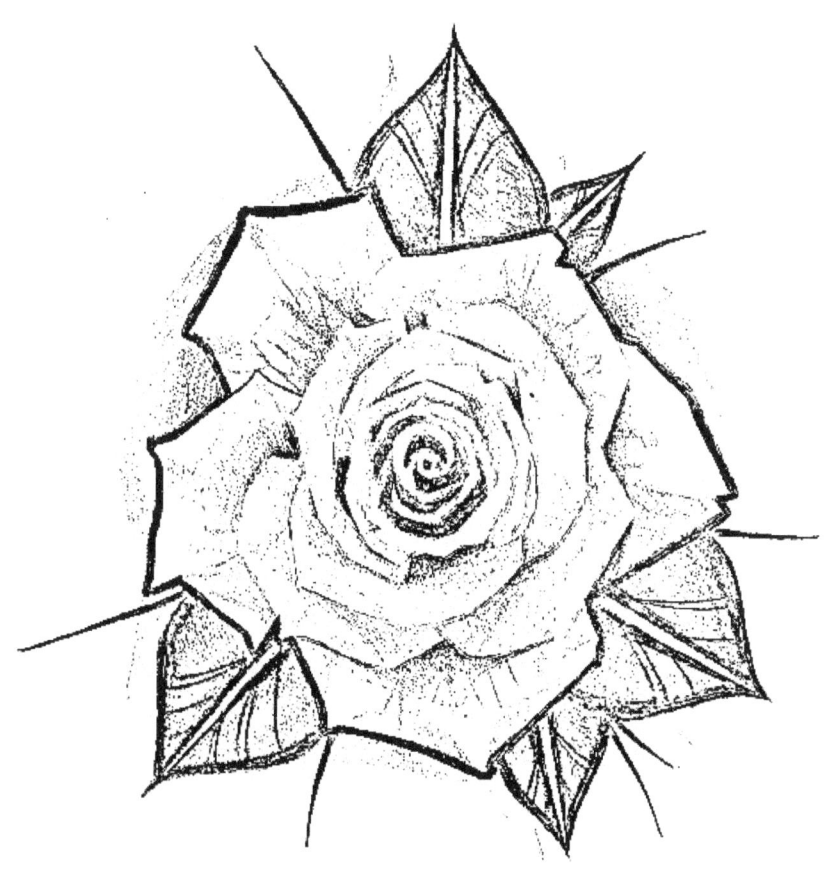

BOOK TITLE

Blank

ROSE 4

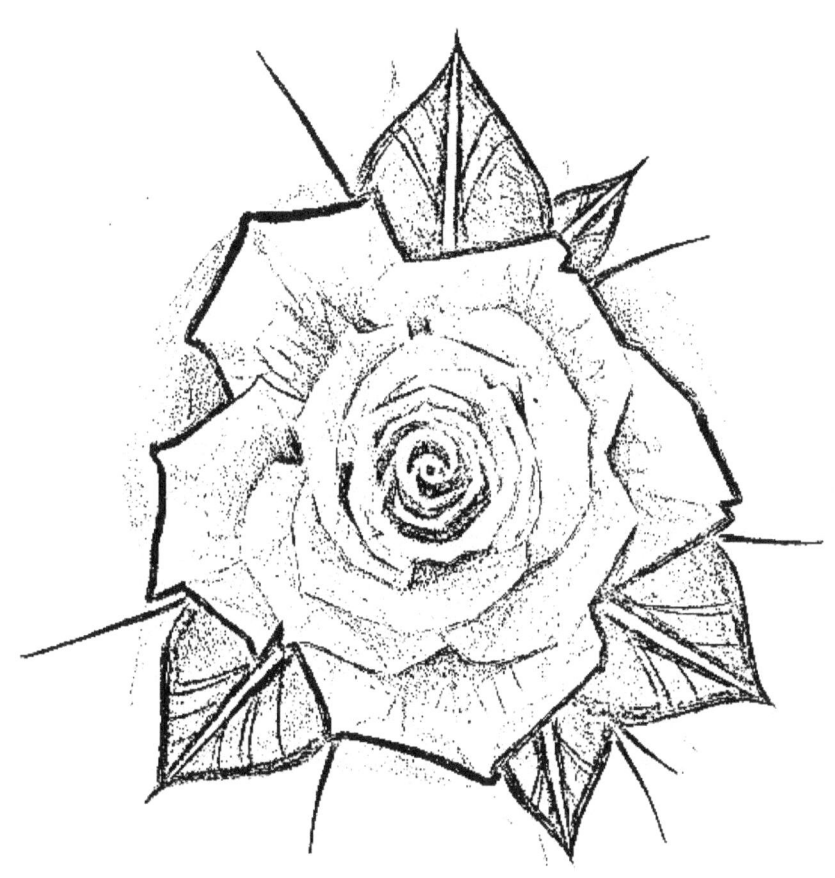

BOOK TITLE

Blank

BOOK TITLE

ROSE 5

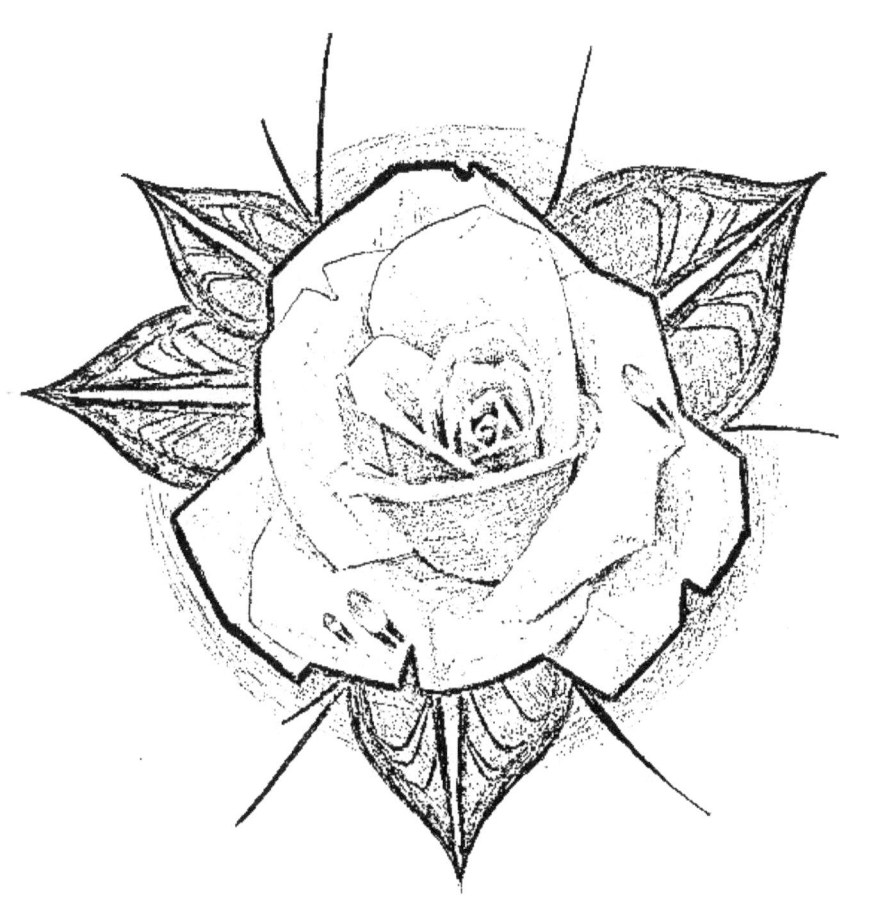

BOOK TITLE

Blank

BOOK TITLE

ROSE 5

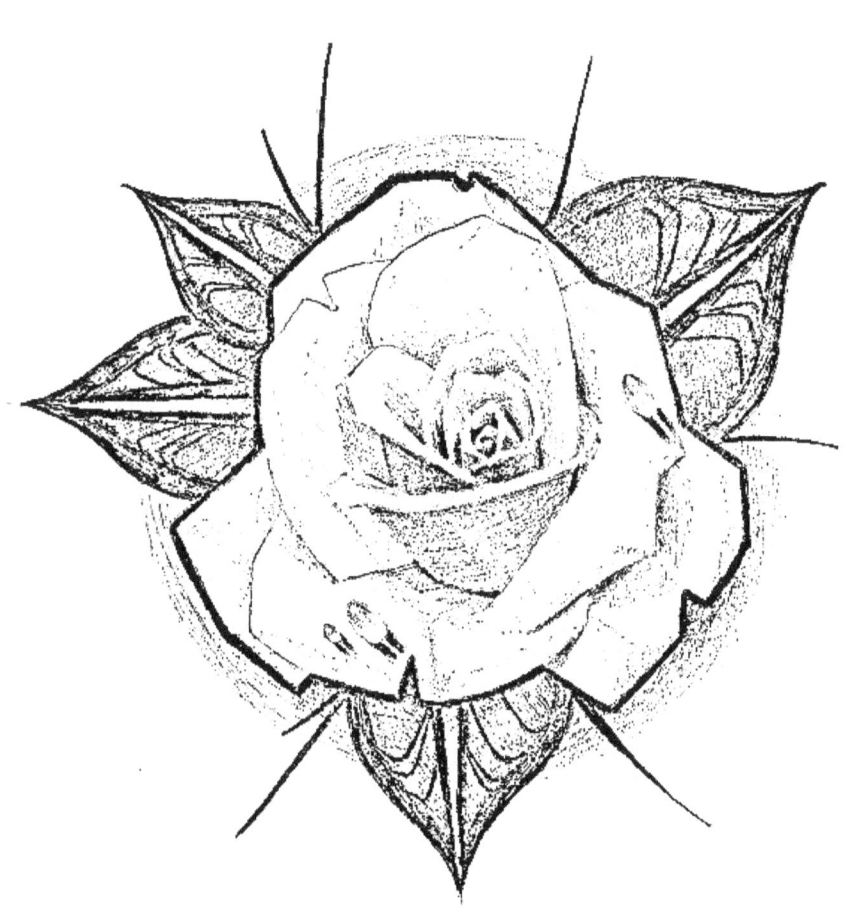

BOOK TITLE

blank

BOOK TITLE

ROSE 5

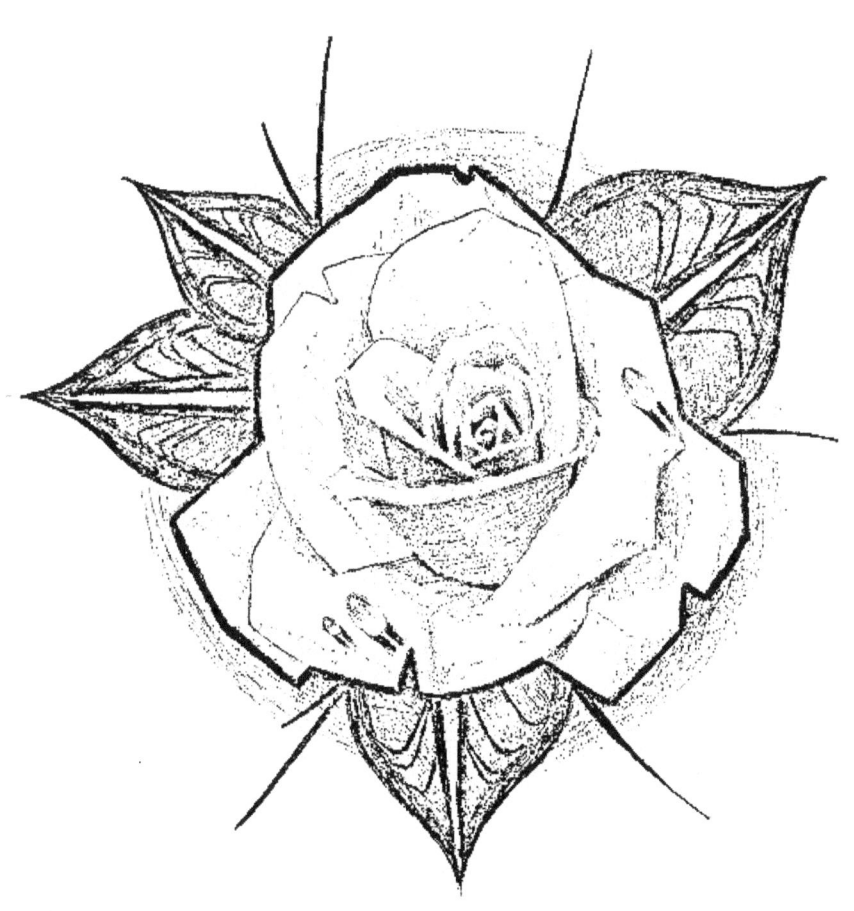

BOOK TITLE

Blank

ROSE 6-12

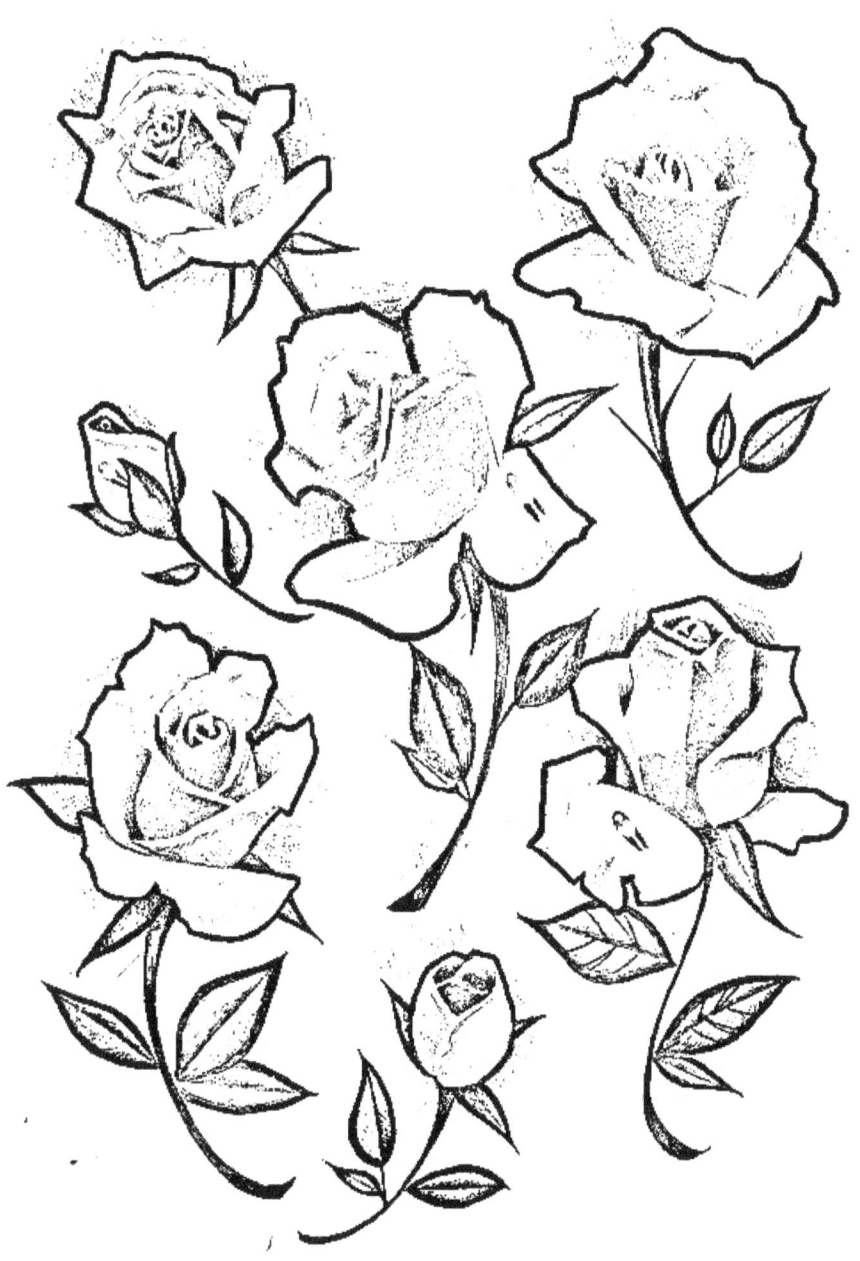

BOOK TITLE

Blank

ROSE 6-12

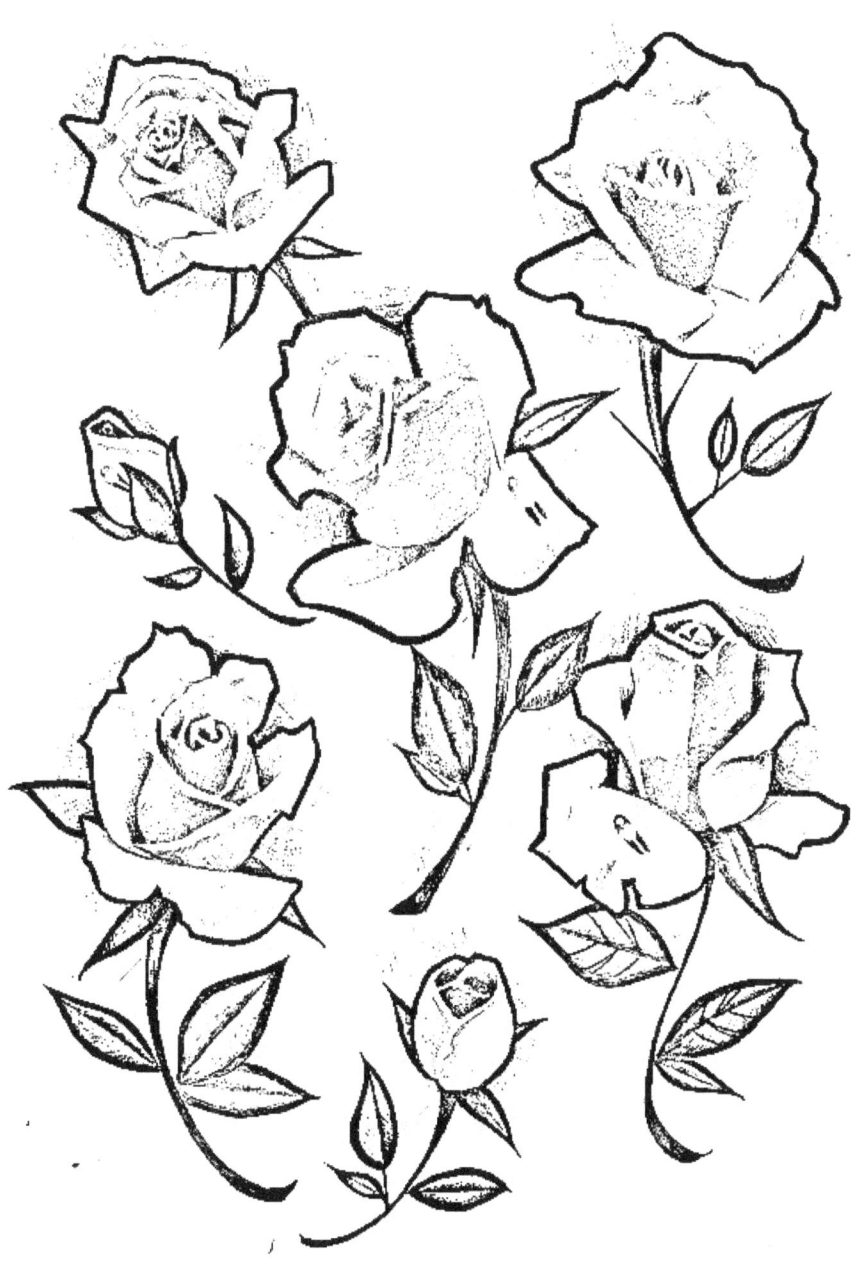

BOOK TITLE

blank

ROSE 6-12

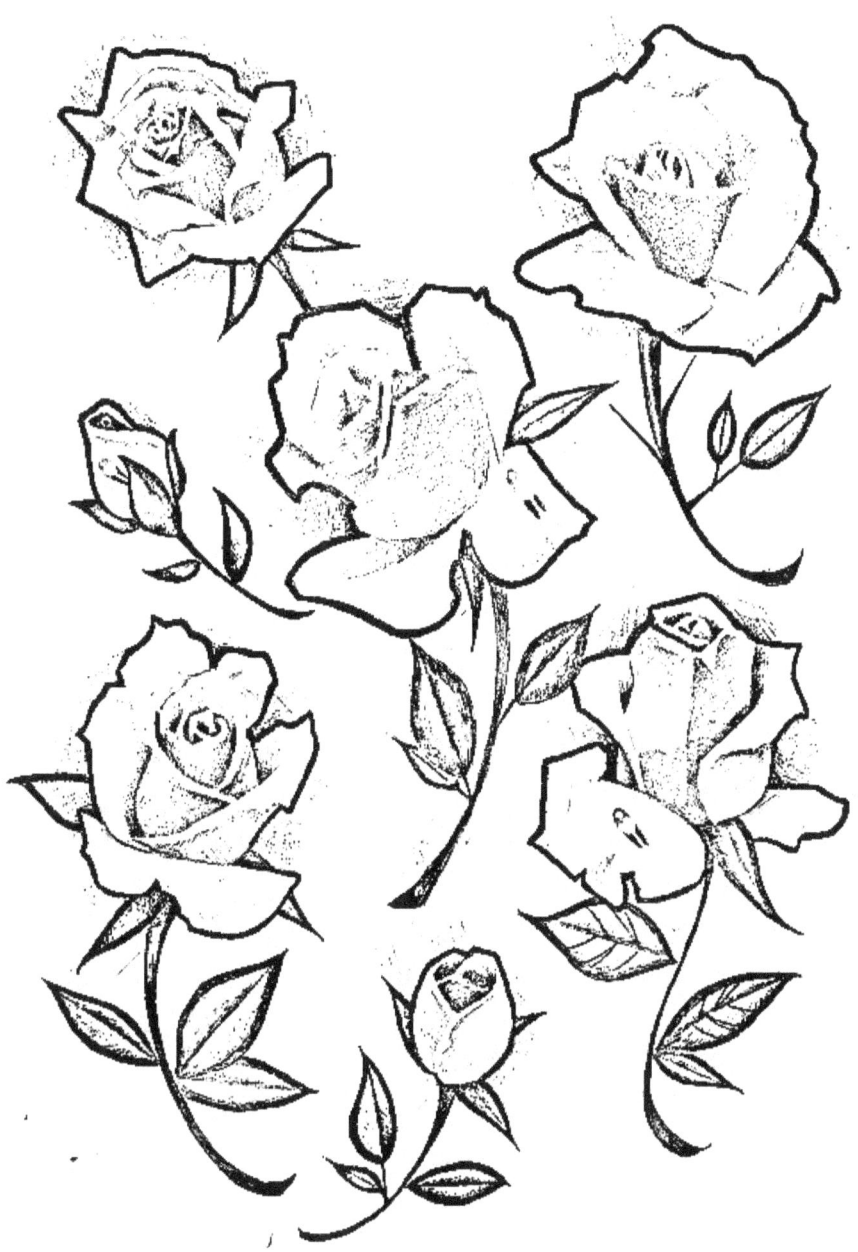

BOOK TITLE

blank

ROSE 13

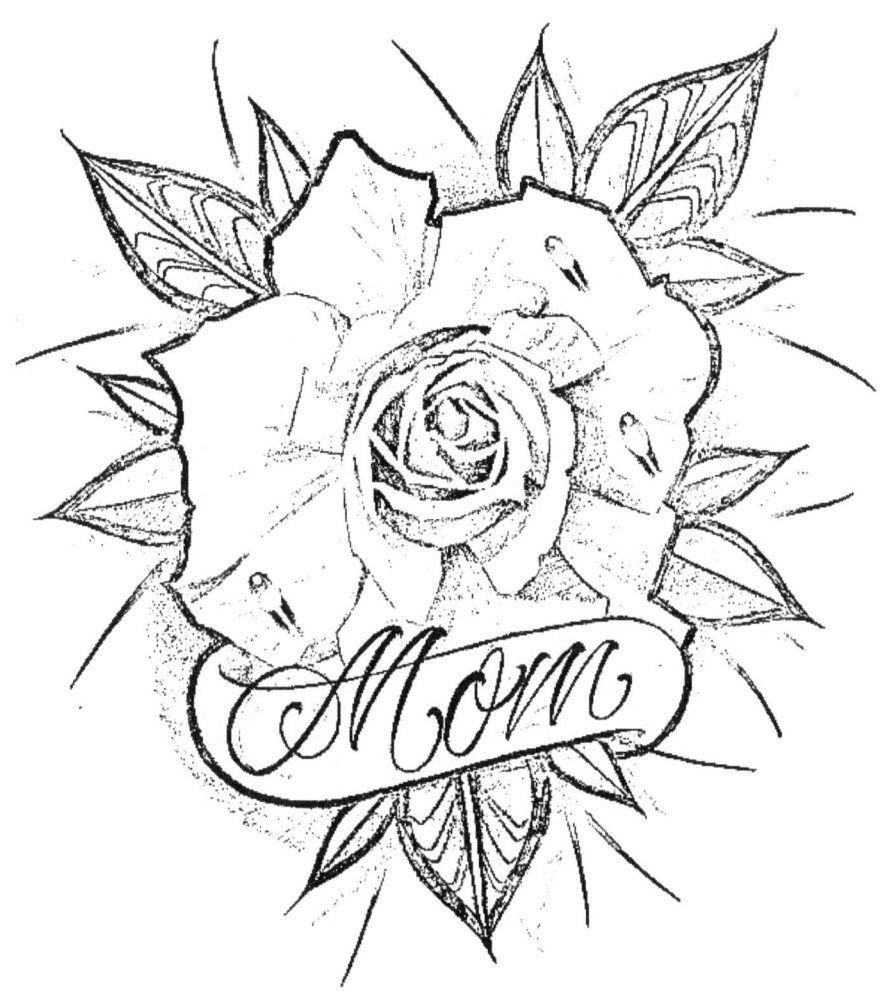

BOOK TITLE

Blank

ROSE 13

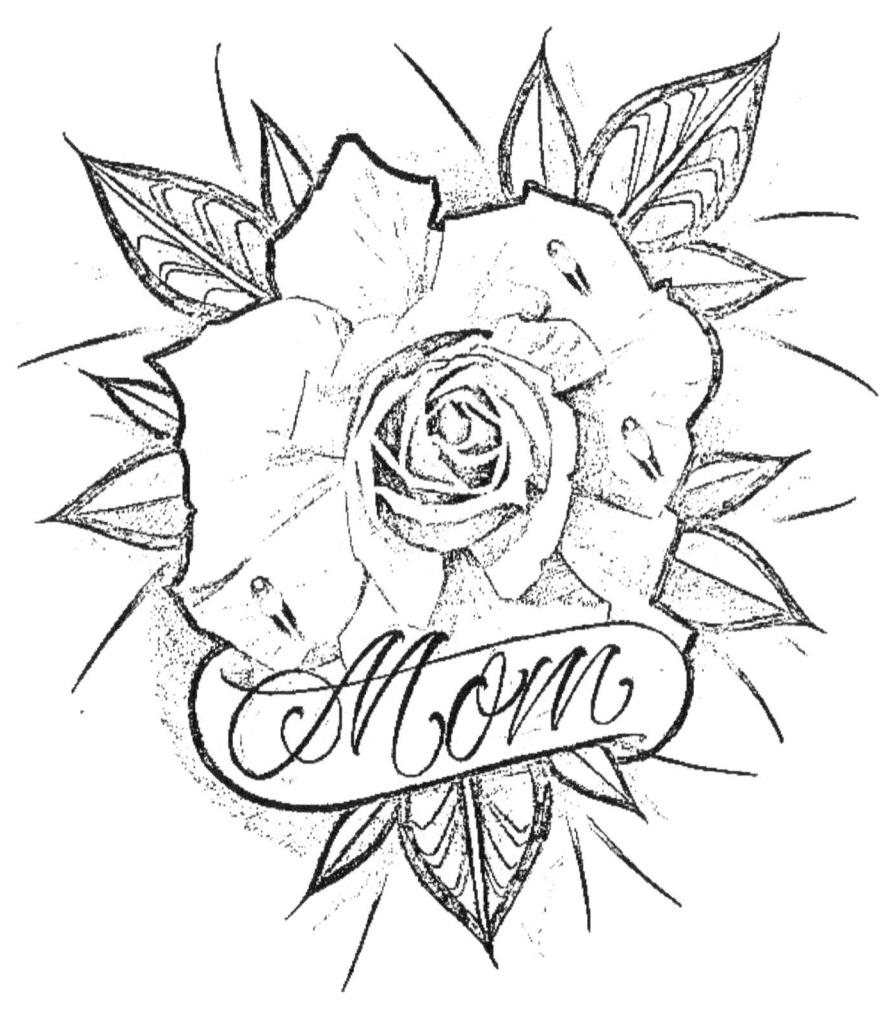

BOOK TITLE

Blank

ROSE 13

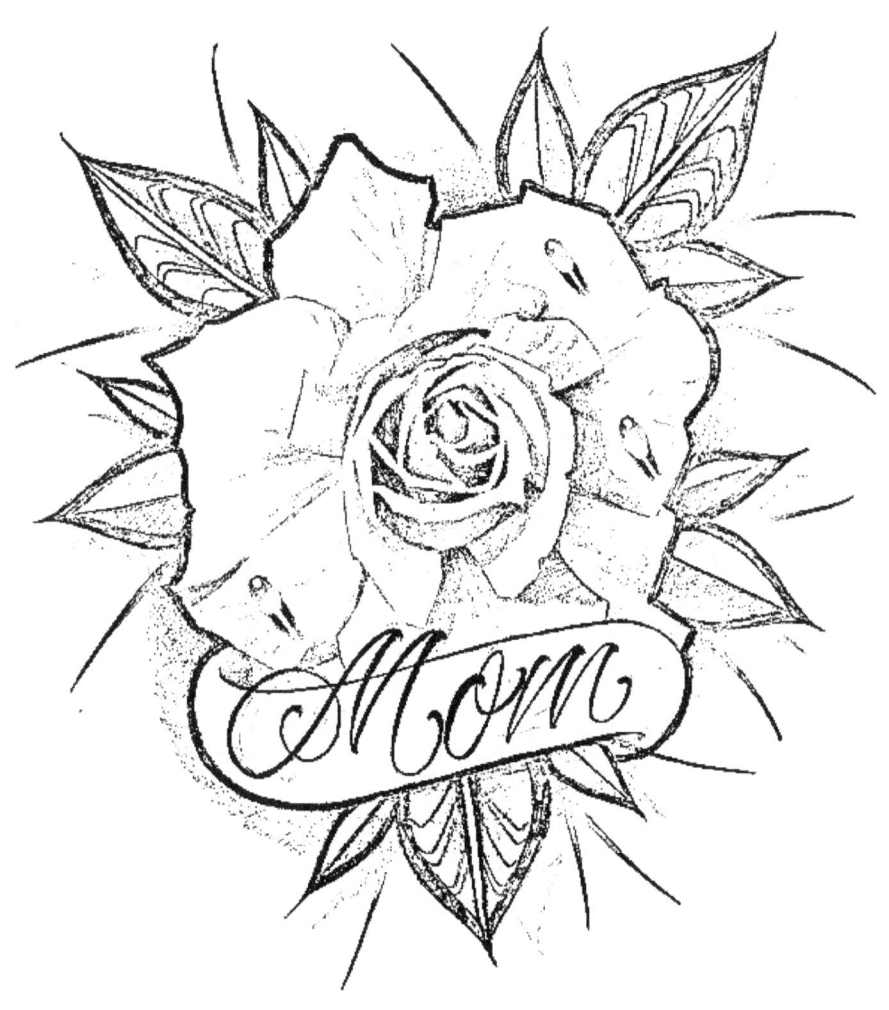

BOOK TITLE

Blank

ROSE 14

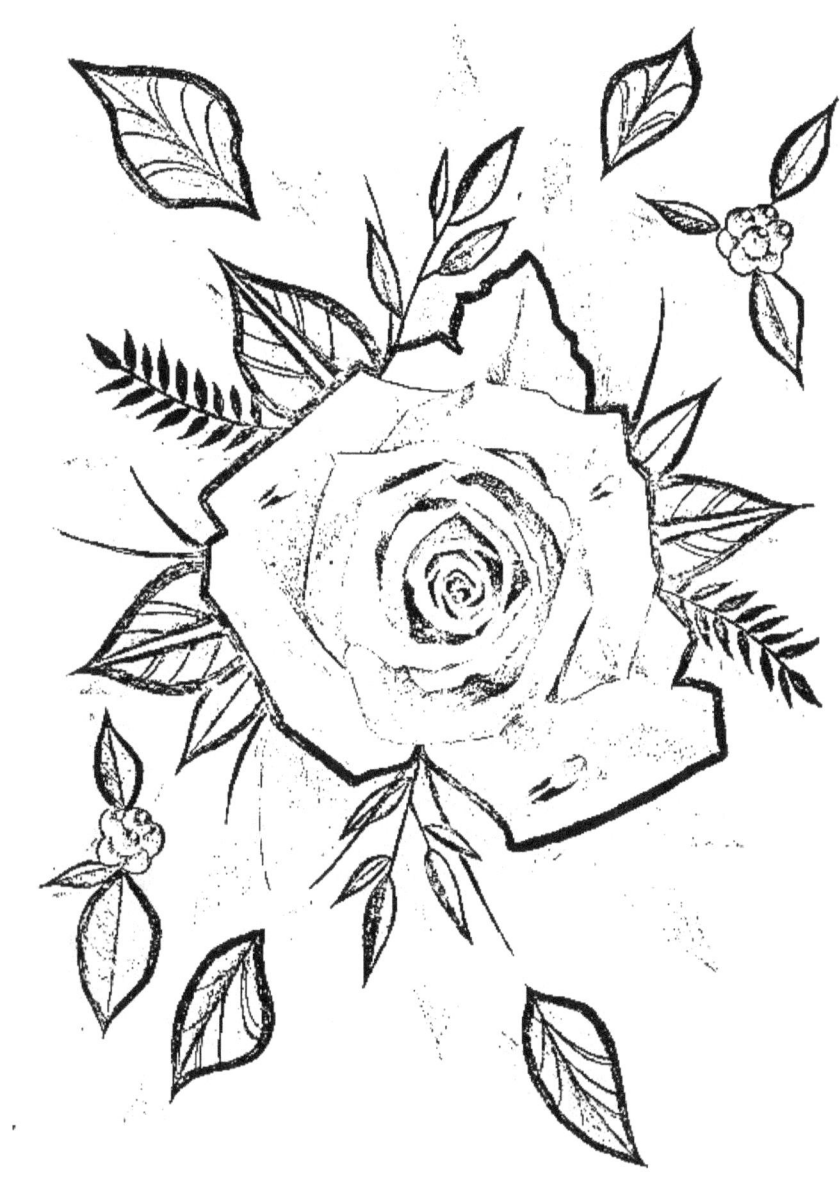

BOOK TITLE

Blank

BOOK TITLE

ROSE 14

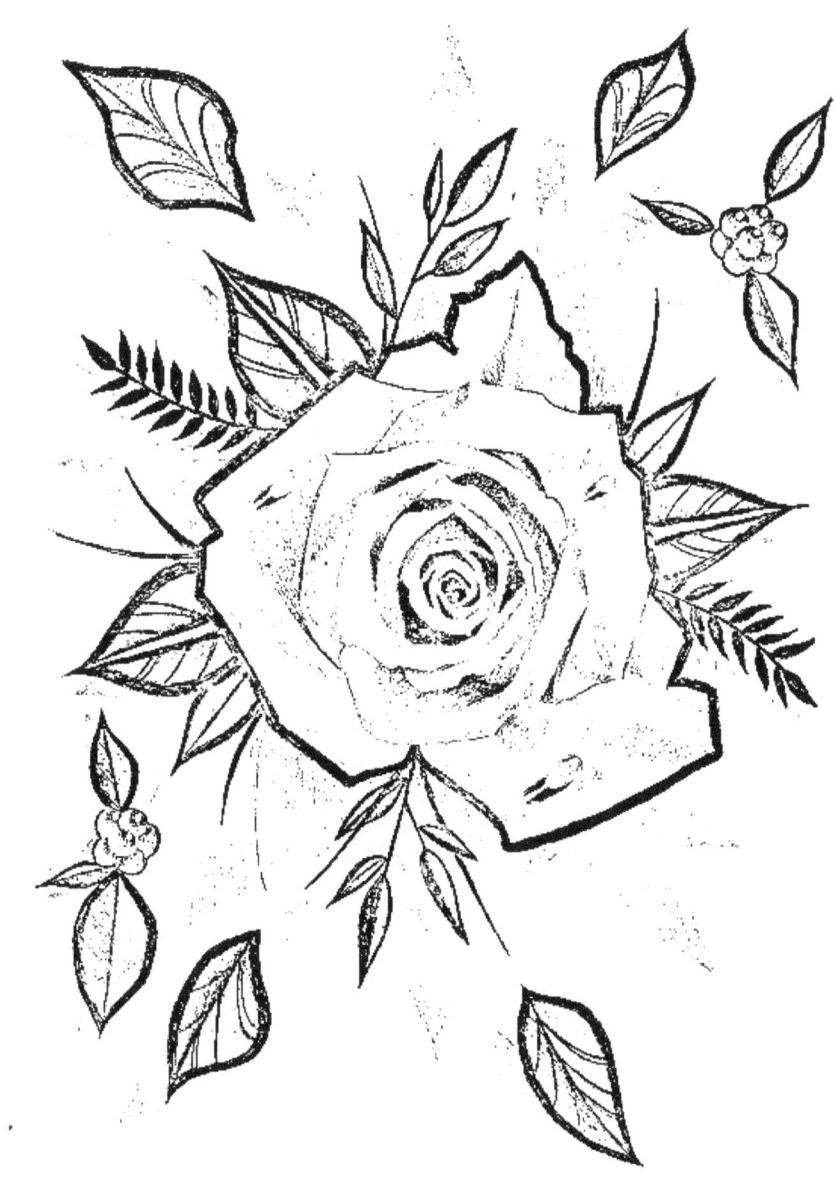

BOOK TITLE

Blank

ROSE 14

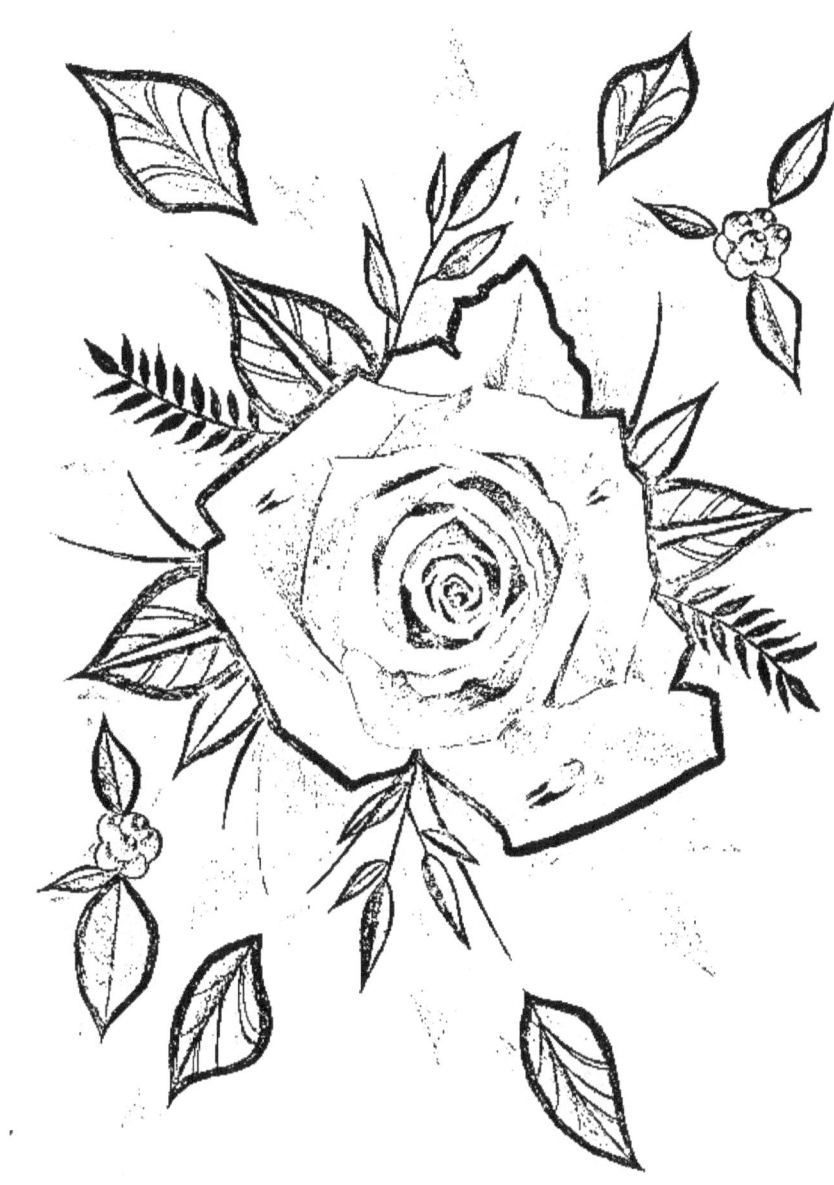

BOOK TITLE

Blank

BOOK TITLE

ROSE 15

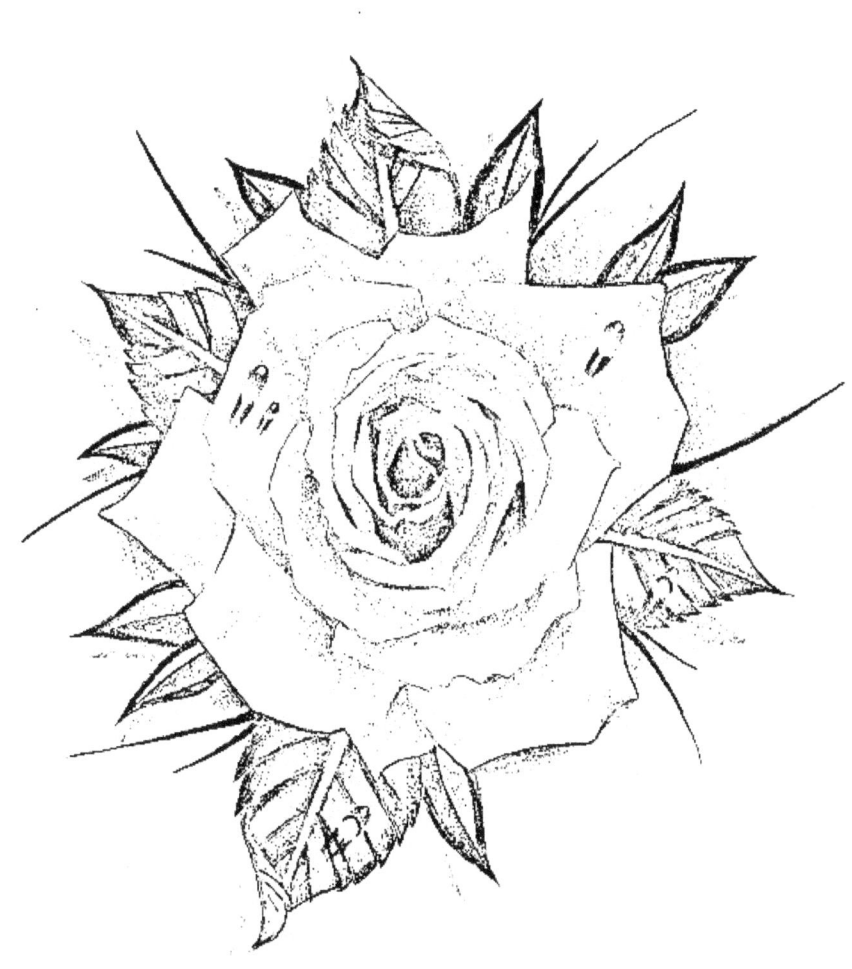

BOOK TITLE

Blank

ROSE 15

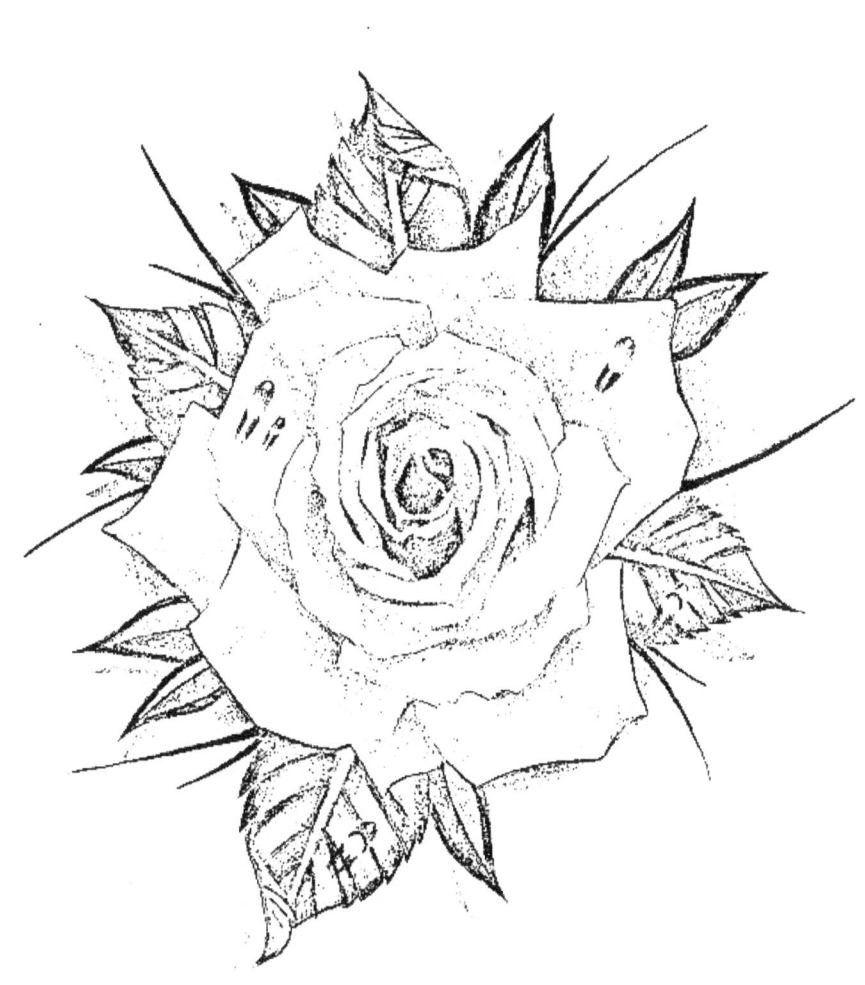

BOOK TITLE

Blank

BOOK TITLE

ROSE 15

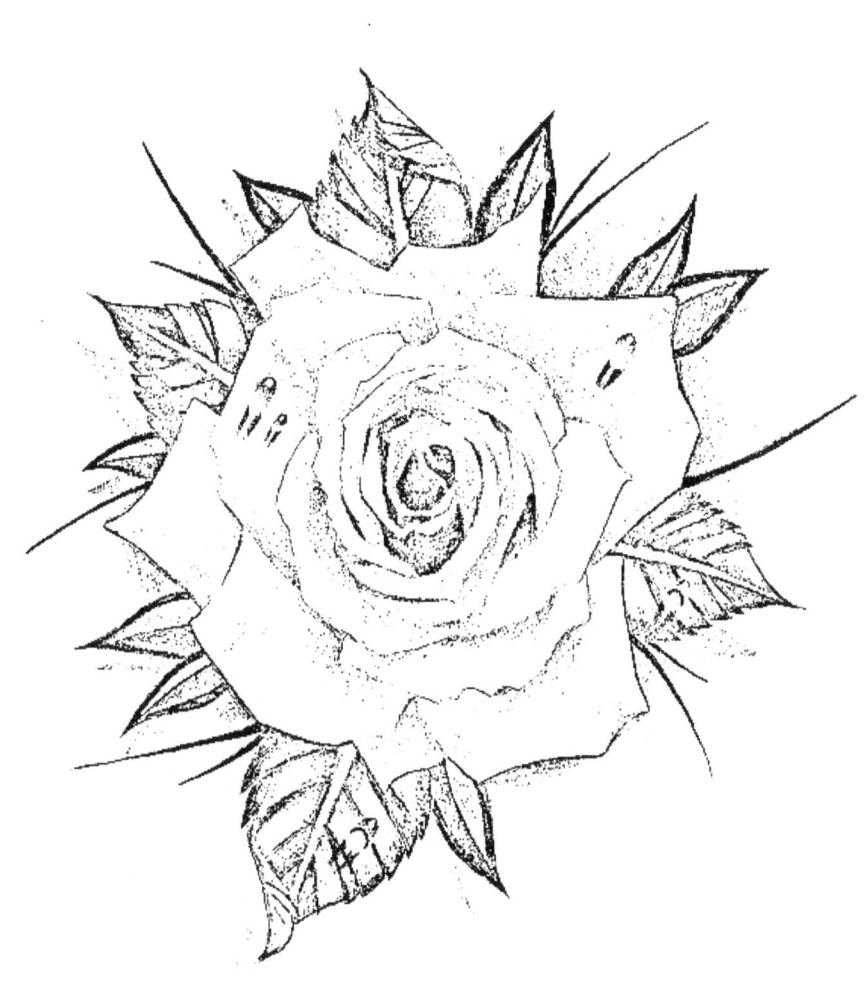

BOOK TITLE

Blank

ROSE 16

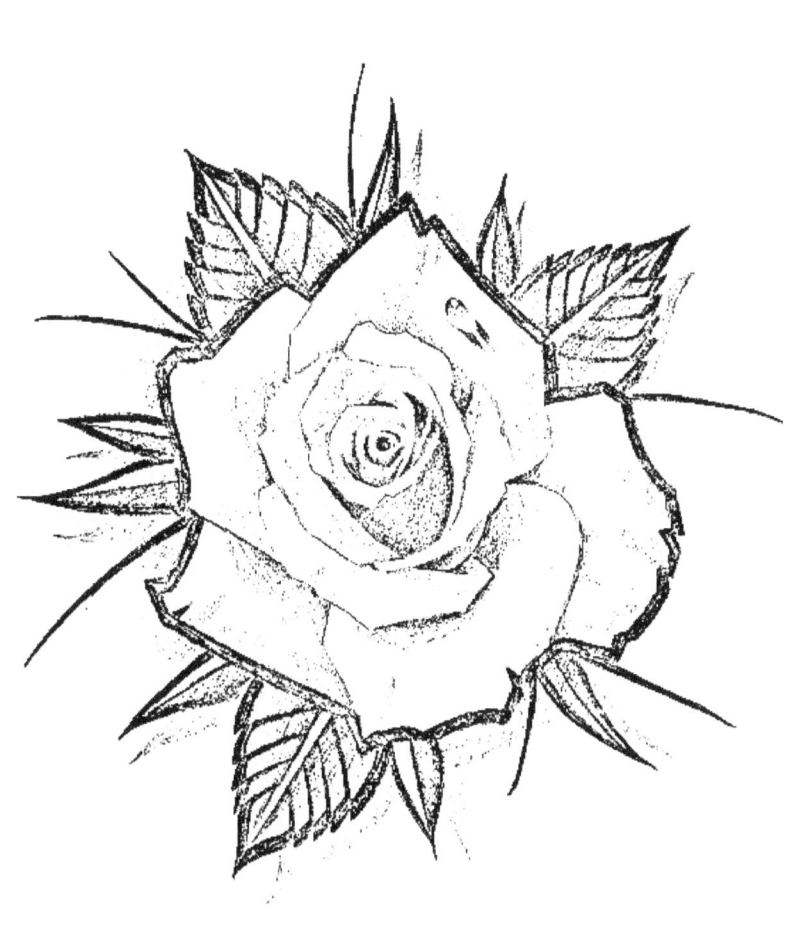

BOOK TITLE

Blank

ROSE 16

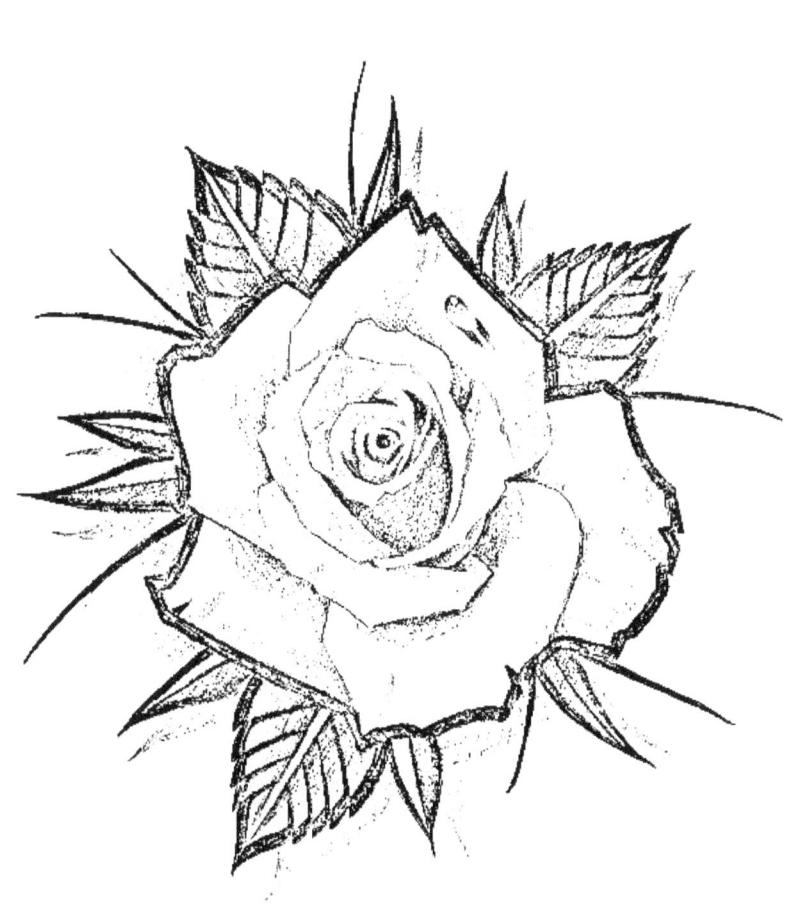

BOOK TITLE

Blank

BOOK TITLE

ROSE 16

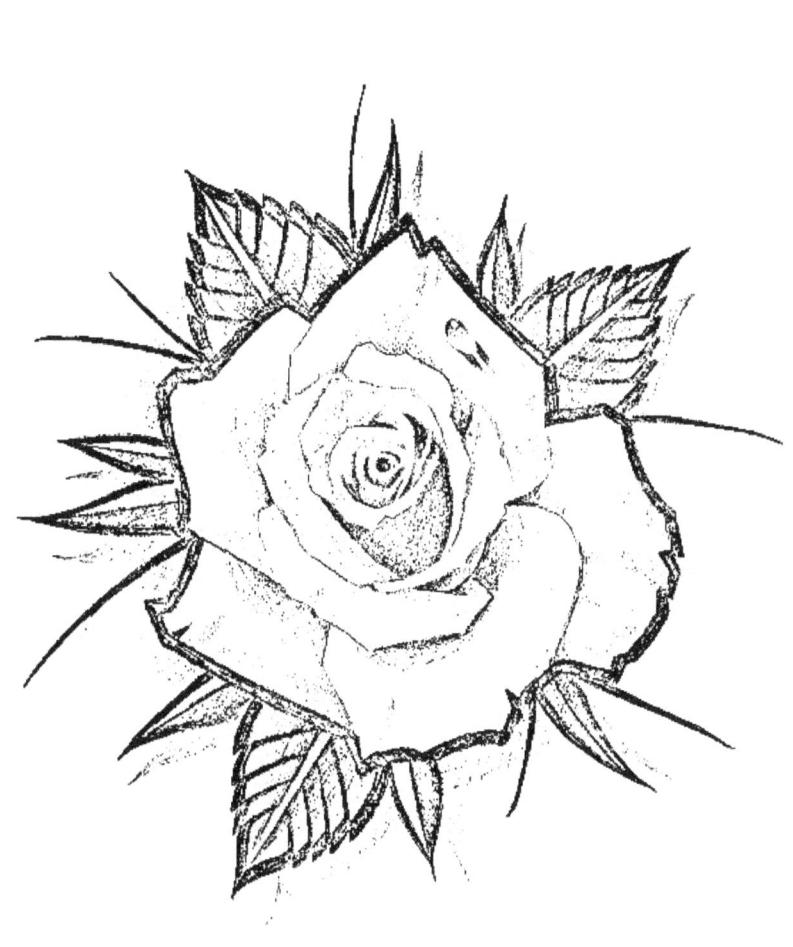

BOOK TITLE

Blank

Rose 17-21

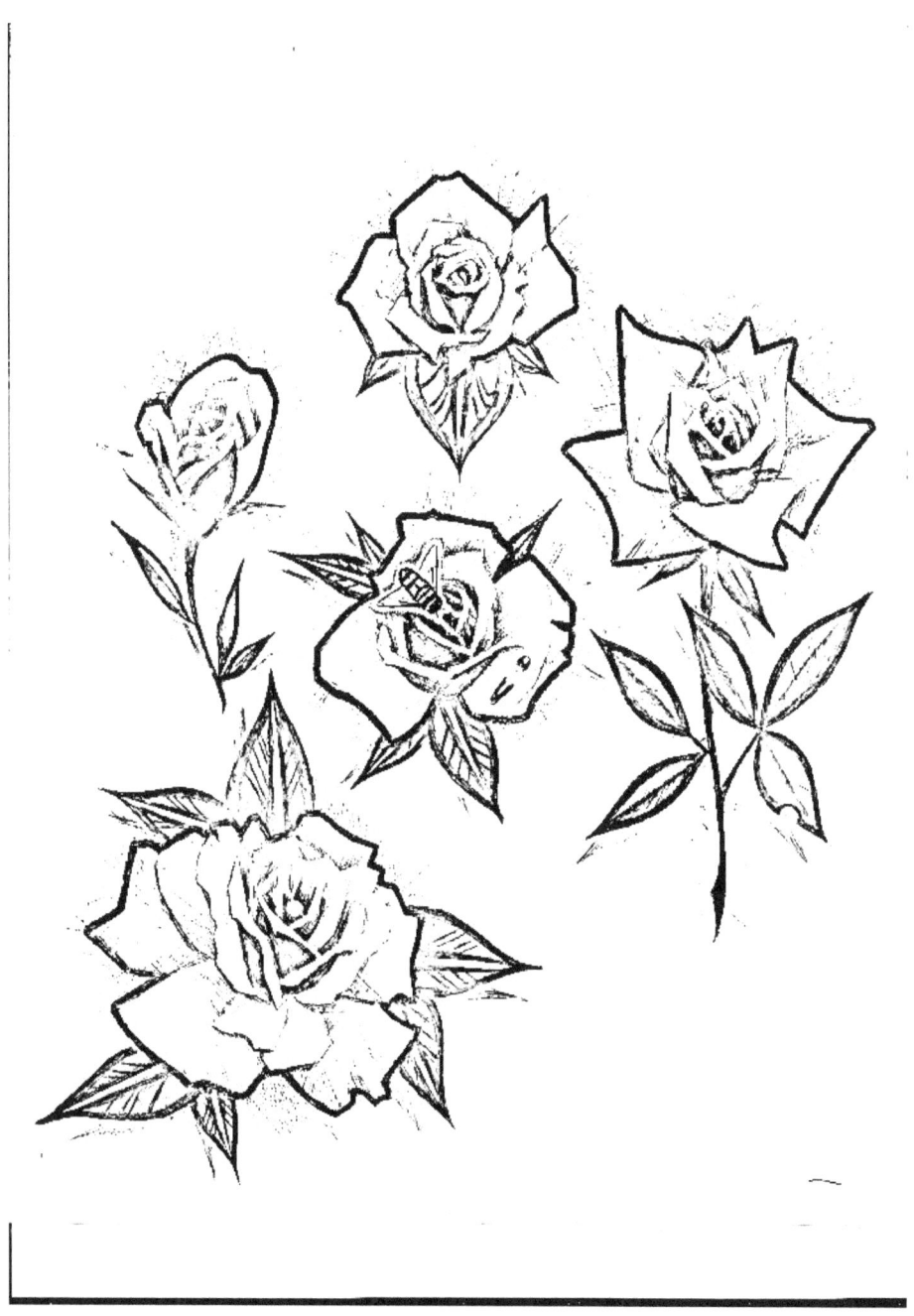

BOOK TITLE

Blank

ROSE 17-21

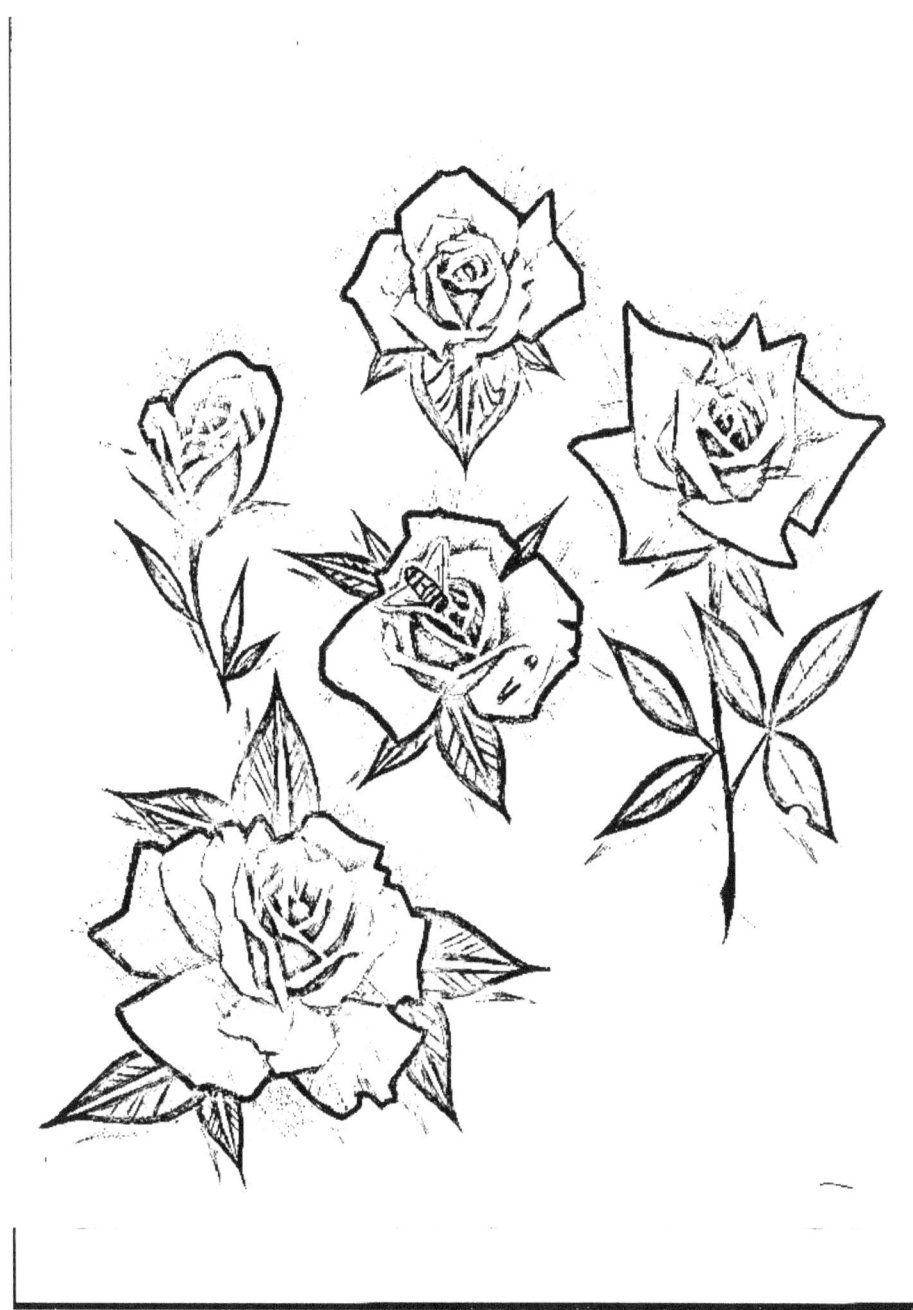

BOOK TITLE

Blank

ROSE 17-21

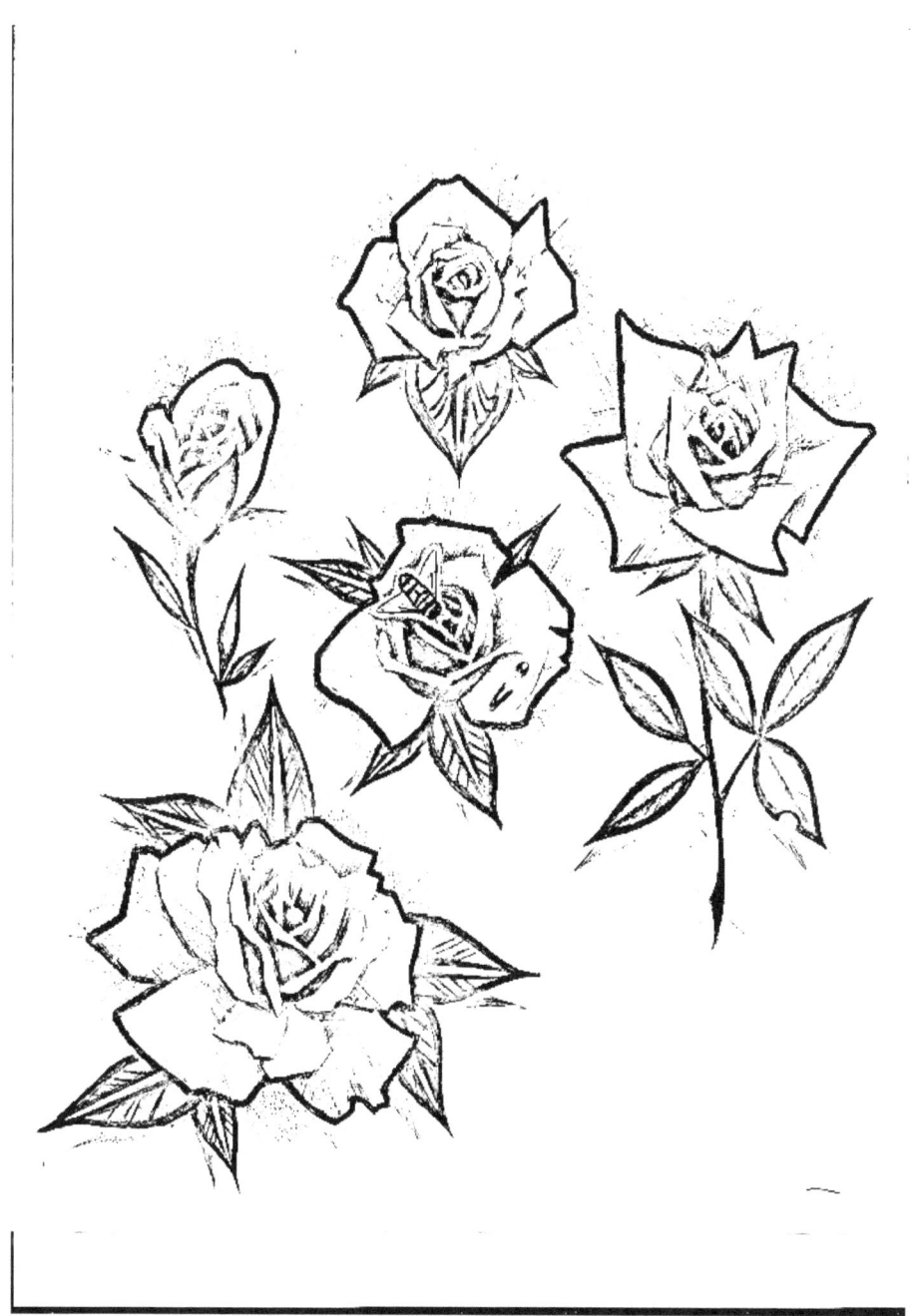

ABOUT THE AUTHOR

Instagram: LeezeyTattoo

www.ingramcontent.com/pod-product-compliance
Lightning Source LLC
Chambersburg PA
CBHW081455220526
45466CB00008B/2662